Reflections of a Glorious Life

Reflections of a Glorious Life

Patrick Nwakamma Ottih

Mazi Ngozi Ottih

To order additional copies of this book, contact:
Xlibris Corporation
1-888-795-4274
www.Xlibris.com
Orders@Xlibris.com
49119

Contents

COMMENTARY

This text is in remembrance of the many who labored to salvage the honor of the Igbo and all those who died in the battle of Biafra. And to all the friends of the Igbo, who recognized the Republic of Biafra or aided the republic in other forms.

Listed are a few of the friends of the Igbo:

The Republic of Cote D'Voire, the Republic of Gabon, the Republic of Tanzania, the Republic of Zambia, the Republic of Haiti, the Republic of Israel, the Republic of France, the Republic of Portugal, the United States government of Richard Nixon, the West Cameroon regional government.

Forward

Chief Patrick Nwakamma Ottih (1918-November 18, 2004) was a Nigerian citizen of the Igbo ethnic population in Eastern Nigeria, who contributed significantly in the African Nationalist Movement, with contemporaries such as Abdul Nasser of Egypt, Kwame Nkrumah of Ghana, and Sokou Toure of Guinea. He also participated in the Southern Cameroon independence struggles, the Igbo State Union, the Biafran Movement/secession struggles and the Nigeria-Biafra war.

He relocated to the Southern Cameroon territory in 1932, resided in the City of Victoria (Limbe), furthered his education through correspondence college studies, became a legendary entrepreneur, established a legacy of humanitarian assistance to charitable organizations and community development efforts, and was actively involved in the socioeconomic and political development of the City of Victoria and the Southern Cameroon territory, through his leadership of the Victoria City business community and memberships in the National Council of Nigeria and the Cameroon's in Southern Cameroon, the Kamerun National Congress and the Cameroon People's National Convention.

He despised poverty, was motivated to join causes to help relieve the sufferings of the poor, and was provoked into joining the Casablanca Group of the African Nationalist Movement by the sufferings of Southern Cameroon indigenes who had endured extreme hardship in the hands of British colonial authorities. He was responsible for the upward mobility of many families, friends, and communities and largely regarded as a gentleman because of his conciliatory approach to life.

His participation in the Southern Cameroon independence struggles was goaded by the same desire to help relieve the sufferings of the poor. He was an active member of the Victoria City and Southern Cameroon regional chambers of commerce and played a distinctive role in the revitalization of the Victoria City down beach business district, all of which was born by his desire to restore the environment and improve the economic conditions of the citizens.

He took up the mantle of Igbo leadership in the Cameroon Republic and served as the president of the Cameroon branch of the Igbo State Union, a branch of a conglomeration of Igbo ethnic organizations led by the famous Nigerian nationalist Chief Dr. Nnamdi Azikiwe.

He led the Biafran Movement in the Cameroon Republic, successfully rallied the Igbo ethnic population in the Cameroon territory to support the Biafran war efforts, and secured the support of the West Cameroon regional government for the Biafran struggle.

He returned to Nigeria after the war, and bolstered the development of his hometown through community development efforts, instigated the participation of the local community in regional affairs, engineered the construction of a secondary school, awarded scholarships to deserving and low-income students, and encouraged civic responsibilities.

He sustained his humanitarian attributes in Nigerian society, involved in the reintegration of the Igbo's in the higgledy-piggledy Nigerian community, and experienced the traumatizing nature of Nigerian politics before retiring in 1983.

He died on November 18, 2004, at the age of eighty-six.

Portrait: In the last days of the twentieth century

His Birth

He was born in 1918 to Mrs. Ejiatu Ottih and Chief Ottih Okoronkwo of Ndi-onyeagorom village of Aro-Awa, in Oguta local government council, Imo State, Nigeria. He started elementary school at Awomama in Oru—East local government council, but completed at Mbieri in Mbaitoli local government council, Imo State, Nigeria. Additional academic pursuits followed at Aba, Abia State, Nigeria, during his years as a business apprentice to a friend of his father, Chief Joseph Nwakamma of Ndiokwara, Uli, Anambra State, Nigeria. Under Chief Nwakamma's guidance, he initiated business correspondence college studies.

On completion of his business apprenticeship, he took up employment at a production factory in Aba, called CFAO. This company transferred him regularly from one location to another, remarkably for training purposes, which enabled his rapid progression and grossed him several salary increments, but caused further relocations from Aba to Enugu, Makurdi, and finally Port Harcourt, where he completed his services with the company.

Upon his departure from the company, he accompanied a friend to Southern Cameroon with the intent to join the police force; but before his travel, he bought several marketable goods with the goal of selling them on arrival. The profits derived from the sales shifted his interest from the police force and skewed him toward business, and thereafter he changed his mind about joining the police force and went into business.

In his early business ventures, he repeatedly bought the very products that had earned him reasonable profits, but soon realized the dangers associated with distant travels and transportation of the goods to his location: at which point he sought to diversify his trade and attempted to market other products, most of which were not readily available in the local market. This led him to approach colonial government officials who were responsible for issuing importation licenses, at a time when importation was viewed as the exclusive prerogatives of the colonial authorities. It was therefore surprising that the colonial masters assisted him toward this goal. By this action, he had ventured into a division of the colonial structure that was viewed to be completely out of bound for the indigenes of the territory—never mind the fact that he was not really an indigene of the area. It may have been possible that he was allowed this prerogative because he was not an indigene of the area.

Realizing that the colonial authorities were willing to grant him the necessary assistance to obtain importation license, he, for the second time in his business career, rekindled his educational pursuit and correspondence college studies. He pursued his love for education with as much zeal and determination as he had in developing a modern business enterprise; and with that, he overcame his educational handicap and turned out a well-rounded business talent. It is unknown if he actually obtained a degree from his correspondence college studies, suffice it to say that his determination in equating himself with business management techniques facilitated his business enterprise. This was how he acquired the knowledge of importation and became the first African in the British colonial Southern Cameroon to obtain an importation license.

Having achieved this objective, he labored tediously in his business to acquire the necessary funds to be able to import goods from abroad. He started gradually in this process by importing as little as he could, a little at a time, but on constant basis. His ability to develop a feeling for public tastes and provide electronic goods when it was the desirable luxury items was what transformed his businesses, and thereafter he became the recognized business endowment and distinguished entrepreneur in the Southern Cameroon territory.

With the general public expecting him to furnish their electronic needs, he endeavored to satisfy their demands. His businesses were ultimately transformed into remarkably successful enterprises; and his business ventures and practices eventually attracted the attention of community organizations and regional government officials, who requested his assistance in community projects and participation in government contracts. These activities and practices monumentally captivated public interests, propelled his public image, transformed his business horizon, and eventually engorged his popularity, fortune, and fame, and spread his name beyond the Southern Cameroon territory, and into his hometown and surrounding communities in Eastern Nigeria.

Family Life

He was married to Mrs. Grace Obiajunwa Ottih and had eight children, losing three of the children in their early years and the first daughter, Victoria Chinyere Ottih, died in a motor accident in Houston, Texas, United States of America, in 1977. He also married a second and a third wife in accordance with the tradition and convention of his time and had ten additional children.

He was known to have assumed an unusual large role in his traditional extended African family even though he was the seventh son of his father. This could perhaps be explained in that he was the first educated offspring of his family (Ottih Okoronkwo dynasty) and although he grew to be prosperous, he was generous enough to absorb the financial burdens of many of his extended family members.

There was also an additional responsibility of recruiting members of his extended African family to work in his companies, where he would teach them the act of trading and helping them establish in the Southern Cameroon territory, after they had fully mastered the act of business management. In this way, he was able to facilitate the establishment of his extended family members in the Southern Cameroon region and shedding himself the secondary responsibility of extended family burdensomeness and spreading of the responsibilities of family encumbrances.

In articulating this awesome responsibility, Dr. Leonard Okoronkwo Ottih said "In fact, it is known in this local government that the Ottih sons were men of able builders in the Cameroon. It is important to indicate here that it was my uncle, Chief Patrick Nwakamma Ottih who cleared the bushes, cleared and made way for Ottih sons to go to Cameroon and achieved all the great things that could be achieved out there. Indeed, it must be said that the actualization of self-fulfillment of this great man in the Cameroon was quite well known".

These responsibilities coupled with the colonial arrangements of the Southern Cameroon territory, adding to the social structure of the region, led to his assuming of a larger and cumbersome responsibility in the development of the City of Victoria and its business community, leadership of the Nigerian community and participation in the socioeconomic and political development of the Southern Cameroon territory.

Stressing on this fastidious responsibility, His Royal Highness, Igwe Nzedibia Okwuchi of Umuhu Okabia, Orlu, Imo State, Nigeria, said "he was a leading socialite representing an integrating presence for us the Igbo Community and the indigenous community in Victoria City. At the instance of the Biafran conflict, it was not surprising that he played a leading role in helping us organize for the relief efforts towards aid to Biafra and seeking for international recognition for the Biafran cause in Sao Tome and France. The fallout of our war efforts and the consequent incarceration we suffered in the hands of the Cameroonian authority persuaded his return to Nigeria and a commitment to help rebuilt the embattled Biafra. Patrick, we will miss you. I will miss you. You were a pivotal light and support at a time when our adventure through life was a complex of history shaping events and efforts but we simply didn't know it. But perhaps you knew."

In a way, Chief Ottih's family in the Southern Cameroon region was the Igbo community, the general Nigerian community, and the indigenous population, for he was the president of the Cameroon branch of the Igbo State Union, and in that capacity, took control of the situation by his contributions in the Nigeria-Biafra war, and as the leader of the Nigerian community, played a distinctive role by his assistance in the Southern Cameroon political struggles and seeking economic and political relationships with Eastern Nigeria, and by his leadership role in the development of the City of Victoria and its business community and the revitalization of the Victoria City Down Beach District. In all these, he was accommodating the interests of Southern Cameroon indigenes.

The children in their early stages of development

Legends of the Biafran Era and the Efforts of a Man

Long after establishing his African Nationalist credentials and partaking in Southern Cameroon independence struggles, he was drawn into the leadership of the Igbo community in the Cameroon Republic. His role in the Biafran struggle was an extension of his responsibilities as president of the Cameroon branch of the Igbo State Union; but with the prohibition of the union by the Nigerian government of Aguiyi-Ironsi and the need for assistance to the Biafran Republic, he converted the union to the Biafran Movement and engaged in the solicitation of support from the West Cameroon regional government for the Biafran struggle.

Although the entrenched control of West Cameroon politics by former Kamerun National Congress members had waned at the advent of the Nigeria-Biafra war, his socioeconomic and political status remained germane. The politics of the region become enmeshed in political bickering by the involvement of East Cameroon leaders in West Cameroon politics and by West Cameroon politicians bent on courting favors from East Cameroon authorities, and the realization that West Cameroon without a standing army would play a secondary role in their union with East Cameroon. This recognition tended to undermine the regional autonomy of West Cameroon, setting in motion a chain of chaotic reactions, which eventually weakened the government, resulting to regional discord and eventual domination by East Cameroon.

But, even with these difficulties, the urgency of the Biafran situation quickly shadowed the risks of East Cameroon encroachment, coupled with the escalating propaganda of the Biafran government, and setting in motion an element of fear in East Cameroon. These factors were responsible for the almost total absence of East Cameroon gendarmeries in the West Cameroon region throughout the Nigeria-Biafra war, thereby enabling the Biafran Movement to organize and strengthening the will of West Cameroon leaders, who from the onset had decided to assist the Biafran Republic through their support of the Biafran Movement.

With all these factors in place, Chief Ottih was unrestrained in his mission of organizing the Biafran community and assisting the Biafran Republic. His enlistment in the Southern Cameroon independence struggles has now benefited the entire Igbo population and particularly the Biafran refugees that received assistance from the Biafran relief fund.

On one of his several business trips to Europe

It has to be recalled that he was a legendary entrepreneur in the Cameroon Republic and had moved into the political arena by first affiliating to the Casablanca Group of the African Nationalist Movement and enlisting in the Southern Cameroon independence struggles and later by securing the leadership of the Cameroon branch of the Igbo State Union, a unit of a conglomeration of Igbo ethnic organizations that represented the socioeconomic and cultural interests of the Igbo's in the affairs of the Nigerian nation and which engineered Igbo dominance of the Nigerian economy before the Nigeria-Biafra war.

Although reserved and humble looking and hardly perceived as a warrior from appearance, his presence is easily noticeable in a crowd; and time and time again, those who tried to undermine him were easily pushed aside by others who were aware of his humanitarian attributes and contributions in community development efforts, had observed his political astuteness and firmly believed in the fairness of his leadership.

His accommodating approach to life neutralized many who had otherwise seen themselves as rivals and, in some instances, destroyed their little chances by forcing issues that were being handled in the most appropriate ways. This attribute invited goodwill toward him, elevated his political status in the Cameroon Republic and was largely responsible for his common reference to being a classical gentleman by both his business and political associates. He was a politician of a kind, who valued service before benefits, and not because he was rich, but because he firmly believed in helping others and without regard to nationality or ethnic origins. This rear quality was what neutralized his potential Cameroonian enemies who saw him as a foreigner, but had few means of substituting the benefits he was providing to their community.

Although a Nigerian citizen in the West Cameroon region, his friends in the West Cameroon political leadership—such as Mr. Solomon Tandeng Muna, Mr. Augustine Ngom Jua, and Dr. Emmanuel M.L. Endeley, who were the vice president of the republic, the prime minister of West Cameroon, and the head of Fako division of West Cameroon during the Nigeria-Biafra war—saw him as one of theirs and worked with him to sustain the Biafran struggle and save the lives of thousands of Biafran refugees who could have perished in the war.

Despite the encroaching attitude of the Cameroon national government in the affairs of the West Cameroon region, he found the courage to form the Biafran Movement, secured West Cameroon government support for the Biafran Republic, successfully protected the movements naughtiness on West Cameroon soil, hosted Biafran diplomatic delegations at his home, provided adequate accommodations to the Biafran diplomatic staff, and authorized one of his commercial buildings to be converted to a temporary Biafran government secretariat or embassy. He convinced the West Cameroon regional authorities to allow the regional airport at the capital (Buea) to be used as the departing point for Biafran diplomatic missions.

The Biafran struggle consumed the social life of the leaders of the Biafran Movement and languished the economic progress of many of the foot managers and night messengers. The foot managers were the leaders of organized segments of the younger Igbo population, who were responsible for recruiting willing individuals to travel to various Cameroon cities, towns, and surrounding communities to inform Biafran citizens of the work of Biafran Movement and seek their contributions to the Biafran relief fund. The youngsters who participated in these missions were referred to as night messengers or warriors. They were mostly recruited from the City of Victoria, Buea, Kumba, Tiko, and the surrounding communities, and were composed primarily of younger Igbo traders, jobless Igbo youths, private businessmen, civil servants, industrial workers, and much more. They were enthusiastic about the Biafran Movement and relief efforts, and many were eager to return to the Biafran heartland to join the battle.

The movement, although led by Chief Ottih, had the inputs of other Igbo leaders, many of whom participated in several meetings, went on numerous errands, and volunteered time to assist the foot managers in various capacities. These leaders congregate regularly at odd hours of the mornings to engage in discussions among themselves or with members of the foot managers on ways to improve the efforts of night messengers and relief collections. It was at these meetings that the plans of actions and schedules of places to visit was made and decisions were taken to determine who among the foot managers will be charged with the responsibility of co-coordinating the activities of night messengers or warriors to various assignments and forward whatever is collected to the headquarters or secretariat in Victoria.

Although the purpose of the movement was initially that of soliciting funds and materials from Biafran citizens who were resident in the Cameroon Republic, and to use such funds and materials to augment the lives of suffering Biafran refugees who were starving to death as a result of Nigerian government economic blockade against the Republic of Biafra, their mission quickly took a different turn as the conflict intensified and Biafran military victories became dreary.

As the Nigerian military advanced into the Biafran heartlands, Biafran political and diplomatic leaders panicked and scrambled for action. At this pinnacle, Biafran leaders resorted to known points of support and narrated the stories to Biafran diehards and patriots who were already concerned and supportive of the efforts of the Biafran government.

It was at this juncture that the daily routines of Chief Ottih was extensively altered; he extended himself insatiably to accommodate the many Biafran leaders and other concerned Biafran citizens who desperately needed help to carry on various assignments. These leaders were of both governmental and nongovernmental organizations. Most were of nongovernmental organizations that were justifiably concerned with societal or communal problems of humanitarian nature, such as the welfare of Biafran orphans and refugees. Under these excruciating circumstances, he had no options than to accommodate all, and that meant a really demanding schedule. He was forced to spend much longer hours at his office, and that also prolonged the hours of the staff that attended to him; but he always endeavored to visit with all that had come to see him. As the hectic schedules continued, his nights became much shorter, and his days became stretched. He engaged himself indefatigably with the predicaments of the Biafran situation and acquiesced to the wishes of these leaders who were desperate for funds to continue the struggle or assist with other communal problems of the Biafran society. They were all delighted at his patience and willingness to listen to their respective problems, show genuine concern for their collective dilemma, and fund their missions. Their appreciation of his assistance loomed beyond the region.

The political and diplomatic leaders were assured of total support by the Biafran Movement, provided official and residential accommodations, and were free to engage broadly in their missions of sustaining the Biafran struggle or finding lasting political and/or diplomatic solutions to the constantly diminishing chances of the Biafran armed forces. A senior member of the diplomatic staff routinely informed him when necessary at his office late in the evenings or at his residence early in the mornings of the Biafran situation, the needs of the diplomatic staff, and the degrees of their progress.

Judge John Chukwuma Anomnachi, legal advisor and spokesman for the Biafran Movement

As Biafran defenses routinely deteriorated, and more Biafran cities were lost to Nigerian armed forces, major Biafran political leaders rushed to the City of Victoria; and the frenzy of activities forced Chief Ottih to temporary forgo his business activities. Some of his close associates in the movement and especially Barrister John Chukwuma Anomnachi (the legal advisor and spokesman for the movement) were, to say the least, infuriated at the failure of some senior Biafran diplomats to have made progress at critical assignments, which had taken them to Gabon and Ivory Coast—two West African countries that had recognized the Republic of Biafra.

There were indications on the ground, that the commitments made by Chief Ottih to his hosts, the West Cameroon regional authorities, that the West Cameroon region wouldn't be used as a staging ground for Biafran troops was bridged. This matter is dealt with in his biography titled *Beyond the Biafran Shore.*

As Biafran defenses crumbled under the might of Nigerian armed forces, January 1969 and later months were hectic for the Biafran diplomatic staff. The Biafran Movement at that point was perhaps the staunchest ally of the Biafran foreign ministry, and the Victoria-based Biafran diplomatic staff was stunned by the deteriorating pace of the Biafran military, and uncertain of the next lines of actions. There were speculations of several initiatives by leading political and diplomatic leaders, including inviting Biafran-friendly African heads of states—such as Felix Houphouët-Boigny of Ivory Coast, Albert Omar Bongo of Gabon, Julius Nyerere of Tanzania, or Kenneth Kaunda of Zambia—to engage the Nigerian military government in discussions as to find a peaceful ending to the conflict.

These initiatives made no headway, and promptly Chief Ottih was persuaded to fully engage in diplomatic activities and lead an international diplomatic mission—perhaps as a fraught attempt at Biafran diplomatic offensive—which would stop over at several sympathetic nations and world capitals, including Sao Tome and France; and included in this mission were Dr. K. O. Mbadiwe, Chief C. C. Mojekwu, Dr. Chike Obi, Professor Kenneth O. Dike, and a few lecturers of Nigerian universities and/or the University of Biafra, Nsukka.

This period was perhaps the lowliest point of the Biafran Movement. After all the agonizing difficulties, the Biafran Republic seemed to be losing the war. This unbearable quandary sent shivers to many Biafran diehards and prompted rumors all over Victoria City that Chief Ottih had lost his might, and that the notorious Cameroon gendarmerie could invade the city at any moment and he would be in real danger.

Although the rumors did not have substantial bearings at the time—because of the support of the Biafran Movement by the West Cameroon regional authorities—there were considerable uneasiness of the situation, by both the leaders of the Biafran Movement and the West Cameroon regional government.

Nevertheless, the Biafran struggles continued, and suddenly there were jubilations on the streets of Victoria City on the news that Biafran commandoes had captured some Italian oilmen and were advancing to retake the Republic of Benin. Biafran citizens throughout the West Cameroon region were tuned to the Biafran broadcasting service, and the eloquent voice of the popular newsman "Okoko Ndem" could be heard on the streets of the city. Members of the youth wing of the Biafran Movement—meaning the groups called the foot managers and night messengers—and their cohorts staged a massive war dance to celebrate the news on the streets of Half Mile, a suburban of the City of Victoria, an event that bewildered some citizens and got the attention of the regional government.

Notwithstanding the uproar, a delegation of West Cameroon leaders arrived at his office at down beach Victoria to congratulate him on the news of Biafran military victories and headed by his old friend and former prime minister of West Cameroon, Mr. Augustine Ngom Jua.

Mr. Augustine Ngom Jua
Former prime minister of West Cameroon
(Supported Biafran struggles.)

Although there were no more exciting news from the Biafran shore after this episode, the expectations were that Biafran commandoes were waiting for another opportunity to strike. As 1969 dragged to an end, the news filtered in that Biafran military was losing grounds and that Nigerian armed forces were poised to take the remaining cities in the Biafran heartland. It was easy at this juncture to see the perplexity on the faces of the leading members of the Biafran Movement. The Biafran diplomatic staffs that were readily seen going in and out of their secretariat were now very scanty, and there were rumors all over the city that Biafra was actually on verge of imminent collapse.

Mazi Edward Okorie, who had accommodated a fairly large number of the political and diplomatic staff at his hotel in Hausa quarters (Victoria City) at the expense of the Biafran Movement, was now very petrified and repeatedly visited Chief Ottih's office, but, he was conspicuously absent from the city at this phase.

It was unknown if he was on another diplomatic shuttle or simply out of public view. There were speculations of his whereabouts, but it quickly became clear that he had been summoned to the West Cameroon regional capital (Buea) to meet with officials of the government and possibly the prime minister of West Cameroon concerning the influx of several Biafran government officials to the region.

The real situation was that Biafra had actually collapsed and several Biafrans from all walks of life were on the run and some had infiltrated into the West Cameroon region. These included a range of professionals, businessmen, civil servants, university professors, assemblymen, diplomatic officials, teachers, and local tribesmen. There were pandemoniums throughout the Biafran countryside, and the Biafran diplomatic staffs that were operating from their secretariat in the City of Victoria had deserted their offices and were in hidings all over the city and its surroundings.

Mr. Solomon Tandeng Muna, former vice president
of Cameroon and prime minister of West Cameroon
(Supported Biafran struggles.)

Many of these individuals later dispersed to Biafran-friendly African states and never returned to the Biafran heartland out of fear of being victimized after the highly publicized killings of several defenseless Biafran civilians on the verge of Biafran surrender. These individuals preferred to spend their remaining days in African states that had given sanctuary to Biafran refugees. Today, many Igbo's comfortably reside in these countries.

However, Chief Ottih's solitary diplomatic shuttle entailed broad consultations with various West Cameroon leaders, including former officials of colonial Southern Cameroon and West Cameroon regional government, such as Mr. Augustine Ngom Jua and Dr. Emmanuel M. L. Endeley. He also visited Yaounde, the Cameroon capital, and held discussions with his old friend, the vice president of the republic and prime minister of West Cameroon, Mr. Solomon Tandeng Muna. But this visit didn't achieve a breakthrough because Mr. Muna abided to the national policy, which was opposed to the Republic of Biafra.

After all his efforts to control the frightful end of the Republic of Biafra, he returned to Victoria City without a satisfactory ending. The Cameroon national government swiftly arrested him, along with leading members of his movement. The authorities assigned agents of the secret service to incinerate his major commercial enterprise and corporate headquarters at down beach Victoria. His alliance with the leaders of West Cameroon was inadequate to save him. He returned to Nigeria after his release and started all over again, an episode that is contained in his biography titled *Beyond the Biafran Shore.*

Dr. Emmanuel M. L. Endeley
Former colonial prime minister of Southern Cameroon
(Supported Biafran struggles.)

The Biafran struggles were, in every respect, the climax of Chief Ottih's life. By this time, he had attained the status of a business magnate in the Cameroon Republic, a leader of the African Nationalist Movement, a credible politician in the Southern Cameroon corridor, a reputable member of the National Council of Nigeria and the Cameroon's in Southern Cameroon and the Kamerun National Congress, an exceptional leader of the Nigerian community and the enduring presidency of the Cameroon branch of the Igbo State Union, the de facto mayor of the City of Victoria, an influential member of the old Oguta County Council Leaders of Thought in Nigeria, and now the leader of the Biafran Movement and relief efforts amidst its unprecedented assistance to the Biafran diplomatic missions. He had single-handedly engineered a struggle from a distant land devoted to the liberation of his people, the Igbo's of Biafra, and made an astounding accomplishment on that track, an achievement that is now recorded. He is acknowledged as an icon of the Biafran struggle. What greater roles can one play in a lifetime. He did exceedingly well, and his story is now told.

Portraits of an African Nationalist and the Chronology of His Activities

Having earned a legendary status in the Cameroon Republic (1932-1971), he engaged in activities designed to uplift the conditions of the working poor through humanitarian assistance to the socio-economic and socio-political organizations that catered to the welfare of disadvantaged children and debilitating communities. These activities spurred the interests of community groups, business organizations and government entities in his business ventures, which enhanced his business interests and eventually necessitated his participation in the political and social affairs of the Southern Cameroon region, coupled with his already celebrated philanthropic mentality; he became an admired socialite amidst the indigenous population and foreign communities. This was how he got drawn into the political affairs of the British colonial territory of Southern Cameroon and ended up as one of the most celebrated leaders of the Southern Cameroon independence struggles.

With his involvement in the struggle, he became their liaison to the British colonial government of Eastern Nigeria, which was loosely in control of British colonial Southern Cameroon. Although his name didn't became memorable among the general population in Nigeria, the political leadership of the defunct Eastern region of Nigeria, knew him as the Southern Cameroon political representative, the president of the Cameroon branch of the Igbo State Union, and the principal Nigerian leader in the Cameroon Republic.

With Dr. Kwame Nkrumah of Ghana in Rabat, Morocco

He was a participant in the African nationalist struggles (1940-70) through his membership in the Casablanca Group of the African Nationalist Movement and later the Nigerian independence struggles through the National Council of Nigeria and the Cameroon's in Southern Cameroon, the Southern Cameroon independence struggles through the Kamerun National Congress, and the Biafran secession struggles through the Biafran Movement and relief efforts. During the Nigeria-Biafra war (1967-70) he formed the Biafran Movement in West Cameroon and led the Igbo residents in the Cameroon Republic toward aid to Biafra. The movements and its leader accepted a crucial role in the diplomatic activities of the Biafran Republic when the government was unable to fulfill those obligations, and embarked on extensive relief efforts to Biafran refugees in the homeland to counter the effects of Nigerian government iniquitous policy of economic blockade against Biafra.

With Mr. Solomon Tandeng Muna
Former vice president, Republic of Cameroon, and
prime minister of West Cameroon

The history of Southern Cameroon's social, economic, and political developments would be inadequate and flawed without including his contributions in that process. As a leading member of the National Council of Nigeria and the Cameroon's in Southern Cameroon and the Kamerun National Congress, he advocated for greater integration of Southern Cameroon with Eastern Nigeria. He was also the business giant, whose leadership of the Victoria City business community enhanced the economic condition of the region by creating a healthy working relationship amongst the indigenous population, foreign communities, local and regional government officials, and the increasingly Igbo-dominated commercial sector.

These responsibilities facilitated his leadership position in the Nigerian community and the indigenous population, and with that he found it useful to collaborate with the Southern Cameroon political leadership, which was seeking self-government from the British colonialists. When the British government prevailed upon the population to either join East Cameroon or Eastern Nigeria, it became his role in the region as the political leader of Eastern Nigeria extraction to transmit the concerns of the indigenous population to the British colonial government of Eastern Nigeria.

Eastern Nigeria at the time was under the leadership of Dr. Nnamdi Azikiwe as the premier. The British government was later to hold a plebiscite in Southern

Cameroon to decide whether Southern Cameroon (later called West Cameroon) was to merge with Eastern Nigeria or East Cameroon. Throughout this period (1940-61), he worked closely with many distinguished Cameroonians, including Dr. Emmanuel M. L. Endeley, Mr. John Ngu Funcha, Mr. Solomon Tandeng Muna, Mr. Augustine Ngom Jua, and a host of others, all of whom were initially members of the National Council of Nigeria and the Cameroon's. These leaders were also at points, members of the Kamerun National Congress, the political party that supported Southern Cameroon merger with Eastern Nigeria as opposed to joining East Cameroon.

With the decision of Southern Cameroon to join East Cameroon, he continued his normal business activities in Southern Cameroon, but encouraged the rulers of (Southern) West Cameroon to press for self-autonomy as pledged by the East Cameroon authorities during the campaign leading to the plebiscite. This strategy worked—the request was granted, and the West Cameroon regional government maintained a semiautonomous status from their East Cameroon counterpart.

This semiautonomous status enabled the West Cameroon regional government to continue economic and political relationships with both the Nnamdi Azikiwe—and Michael Okpara—led governments of Eastern Nigeria. The relationship brought enormous economic prosperity to Nigerian-owned businesses in West Cameroon, and he was a leading beneficiary of that relationship.

**With Casablanca Group members of the African
Nationalist Movement in Conakry, Guinea**

It was under this fertile climate that the Nigeria-Biafra war erupted. Being well established in the territory, the leader of the Nigerian community, and a political associate of the ruling class, he found an opportunity to help, and succeeded in convincing the West Cameroon regional government to assist the fledgling Republic of Biafra.

He achieved this through the formation of an Igbo-based organization, which he called the Biafran Movement, but commonly referred to as the Biafran relief efforts. The group encouraged Igbo's in the Cameroon Republic to support the Biafran war efforts, and the members labored to collect relief materials and funds from their countrymen and women who were scattered throughout the communities of the Cameroon landscape. The relief materials and funds collected were later taken to the Biafran State and distributed among starving Biafran refugees in the homeland.

The task of managing the Biafran Movement was tedious and time consuming, and laterally took him away from his businesses throughout the later stages of the war. The intensity of the activities also entailed serious involvements by some of his friends, namely, the late Chief Okafor Meng of Abiriba, the late Judge John Chukwuma Anomnachi of Owerri, and the late Mazi Edward Okorie of Aro-Chukwu.

The Biafran authorities requested a secretariat in the West Cameroon region, and he transformed one of his commercial buildings in Victoria City to serve as a provisional Biafran government secretariat or embassy. He also catered to the welfare of the diplomats who operated from the embassy. He secured the support of the West Cameroon regional government under the premiership of Mr. Augustine Ngom Jua, who was a close political associate.

The prime minister, although sympathetic to the Biafran State and supportive of the Biafran war efforts, was cognizant of the official policy of his national government, which was in support of the federal government of Nigeria. His support must not have been without the knowledge of Mr. Solomon Tandeng Muna, who was both a political ally and a friend to Chief Ottih, the majority leader in the national *parliament,* but later became the vice president of the republic and prime minister of West Cameroon.

Both Mr. Solomon Tandeng Muna and Mr. Augustine Ngom Jua were former members of the Kamerun National Congress, the party that received generous support from him during their struggle for independence, and members of the National Council of Nigeria and the Cameroon's in Southern Cameroon. These leaders thought it prudent to return the favor and support the efforts of their friend in his dire moment, and to help liberate his people from the potent hands of Nigerian military government.

It should be noted that the West Cameroon regional government was of enormous help to the Biafran Republic, and her willingness to allow relief materials across their border to feed starving Biafran refugees in the homeland safeguarded the lives of millions of innocent Biafran citizens who could have perished in the struggle. Chief Ottih's achievements in securing the support of the West Cameroon regional government, dedication to the Biafran relief efforts, and commitments to the diplomatic activities, accentuates his devotion to the Biafran struggle.

**With members of the National Council of Nigeria and the
Cameroon's in Southern Cameroon**

West Cameroon was a fertile ground for the Biafran relief efforts; and several notable Biafran political and diplomatic leaders, such as Chief C. C. Mojekwu, Dr. K. O. Mbadiwe, Dr. Chike Obi, Professor Kenneth O. Dike and a host of others, who were part of the Biafran government political and diplomatic delegations at various stages of the war, depended upon his support and that of his movement as the fiber or pillar for their assignments. The presence of Chief C. C. Mojekwu, a close associate of the Biafran leader, the Biafran minister of internal affairs and former Biafran attorney general and minister of justice, was the verification that Chief Ottih and his movement needed to validate that the Biafran government was aware of their efforts and valued their contributions. His financial contributions to the war efforts amounted to millions of Cameroon francs. His support for the diplomatic activities of the Biafran government earned him a lot of admirations—from the Igbo community in Cameroon, the Biafran political and diplomatic leaders that undertook diplomatic activities on behalf of the Biafran State, as well as from the West Cameroon regional authorities that supported the Biafran struggle.

Despite his obligations to the movement and the need for his continuous presence in the region, he was persuaded to lead a Biafran diplomatic delegation on a tour of world capitals seeking recognitions for the republic. This was at the critical stages of the war, and among those with him were Chief C. C. Mojekwu, Dr. Chike Obi, Dr. K. O. Mbadiwe, Professor Kenneth O. Dike, and a few lecturers of Nigerian universities and/or the University of Biafra, Nsukka

As the Nigeria-Biafra war was winding to an end, the influx of several high-ranking Biafran government officials and others to West Cameroon was of colossal concern to him, and he labored to calm the fears of the West Cameroon regional authorities that had supported the Biafran struggle.

At the conclusion of the war (1970), the Cameroon national government was swift to arrest him along with leading members of his movement. The authorities capitalized on the demise of the Biafran State to extract exorbitant amounts of money from the detainees. During their time in detention, a group of his former colleagues in the Kamerun National Congress pressured their government for his freedom; and Chief Okafor Meng of Abiriba, a close friend and fellow detainee, risked his own safety by speaking out against government attempts to isolate him. The authorities indicated their abhorrence of him by incinerating his corporate headquarters in down beach Victoria.

The Cameroon national government was so gravely infuriated by the support of the West Cameroon regional government for the Biafran Republic that they altered the structure of their entire government, abolished the autonomy of the West Cameroon regional government, divided their country into several provinces, and eliminated the elections of provincial governors.

With Kamerun National Congress members and Southern Cameroon leaders in Buea

Despite the support of Alhaji Ahmadou Ahidjo, the Cameroon president, to the Nigerian government, he was soon hoaxed into resigning from the presidency of his country on account of ill health, and the Nigerian government paid no attention to the predicaments of his family. His successor, President Paul Biya, exiled him and refused his body to be flown home for burial after his death.

Chief Ottih returned to his Biafran homeland (1971) soon after his release from detention on the advice of his friends who feared for his life.

These friends were also the former rulers of West Cameroon, with whom he shared memorable times. They still valued his friendship despite their removal from office on account of their support to the Biafran Republic. He retained a lasting appreciation for their friendships and contributions to the Biafran struggle and regarded them as proven and worthy friends of the Igbo's.

On his return to Nigeria, he initiated several business ventures, but his business achievements were relatively limited, partly due to the unruly nature of Nigerian businessmen and his involvements in the grassroots campaign for the empowerment of the Igbo's in a united Nigeria and the development of his hometown.

Regardless of his disappointments at the degree of dishonesty and disorder in Nigerian society as a whole, and the political class in particular, he maintained his focus on helping to rebuild his embattled Igbo homeland. In 1976, after the Nigerian military government lifted the ban on politics, he was among the founding members of Club 19, an association of former members of the defunct National Council of Nigeria and the Cameroon's. This group joined with others to form the Nigerian People's Party.

In 1977, he was appointed a councilor in the old Ohaji/Egbema/Oguta Local Government Council by the Imo State government and was a candidate to lead the council; but for the unscrupulous nature of a political enemy, he could have emerged the winner. In 1979, his attempt to secure the nomination of his party to the state's house of assembly, witnessed an open hostility by same political adversary—an event that splintered the leadership of the party and affected the personnel's of government, and subsequently led to the disarray of the party at the later stages of the second republic.

With European trade representatives in Buea

In 1983, as governor Mbakwe battled Chief Okafor's attempt to retain the chairmanship of the state's branch of the party, he led his people away from the troubled Nigerian People's Party and into the National Party of Nigeria, where he was made the party's trustee member in the old Imo State and its candidate to the state's house of assembly. Even in his old age, he remained active in the development of his hometown; and in 1987, he formed the progressive welfare association in Awa community, through which he awarded scholarships to deserving and low-income students of Awa Community Secondary school, a school he had founded and actively supported in its missions.

He retired from politics in 1983, but remained committed to the welfare of the Igbo's of Biafra. His role in life had been precious and priceless, a sequence of dedication to noble causes, a compassion for the poor, a devotion to the progress of the family and the community, a fountain of generosity to humanity and of genuine concern to the welfare of the general Igbo population.

He died on November 18, 2004, at the age of eighty-six, after a lengthy illness.

He is remembered for his activities in the African Nationalist Movement, his leadership role in the Southern Cameroon independence struggles, his role as the leader of the Cameroon branch of the Igbo State Union and the Biafran Movement, his relentless struggles toward the survival of the Republic of Biafra and relief efforts, his aid to Biafran orphans and refugees, his assistance to the Biafran Movement militant wing, his contributions to the Biafran diplomatic missions, and his commitment to the general welfare of the Igbo population, which persuaded his involvement in the Nigeria-Biafra war and his return to Nigeria to help rebuild his embattled Igbo homeland.

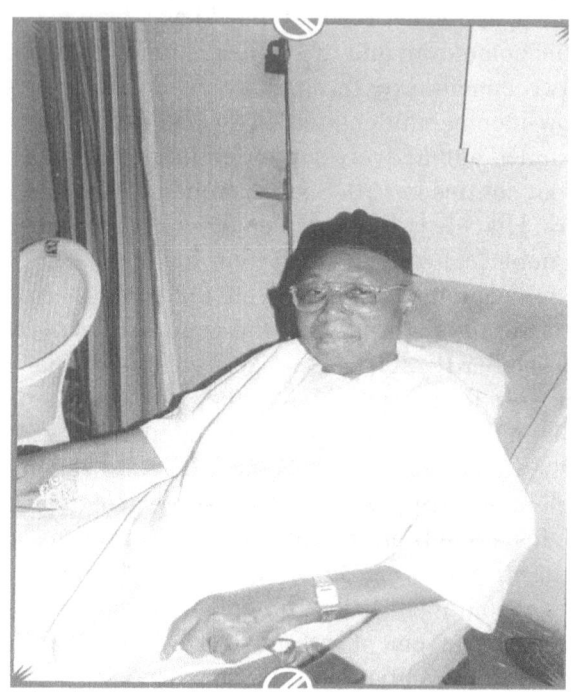

Life is like the wind that blows across the earth because each person lives at his or her own time, but memory is an enduring part of the human spirit and very few are able to erase it from their souls; and if and when they do, they are oftentimes not the same persons again.

Recognize those that made a difference, and maybe others will acknowledge yours as well.

Skyscrapers don't live through the ages of time, but history has for ages, honored those that deserve a spot on its part; and so this one is ranked among the great due to his contributions in the African Nationalist Movement, the Southern Cameroon independence struggles, the Biafran Movement/secession struggles, and his humanitarian assistance to the Igbo's of Biafra, who today have spread to the corridors of West Africa, and may rightly be referred to as the Igbo's of West Africa.

Some Inherent Characteristics of the Igbo Culture and Instances of Pragmatism and Determination of Leaders of the Old

With Chief Okafor Mang and members of the Biafran Movement in the early stages of the Nigeria-Biafra war

As an adolescent growing up in the Cameroon Republic's City of Victoria in the home of the president of the Cameroon branch of the Igbo State Union, Chief Patrick Nwakamma Ottih, I was exposed to oodles of Igbo community meetings and leadership conferences. I neither thought much of the meetings at the time nor had a sense of understanding of the reasons for the meetings, but simply attended to the group at various times as they gather to discuss the affairs of the Igbo's. But one thing I knew for certain was that there were no levies on the members. The leader of the group in whose home the meetings were held always informed the clerks who managed his stores, of the meetings, and to arrange for assorted drinks for the members. The leader was a wealthy entrepreneur and a distributor of beverages among other businesses. It was not unusual for a meeting to be held in the absence of the leader, only that a close relative of the leader had to be present during the meetings.

Many of the members were local traders, and some were trade practitioners and of other professions. Some of the traders were customers of the leader who was into wholesale trading. The leader didn't know who among the members were his customers—except in few cases where the clerks could not provide the needed help would arrangements be made for the customer to visit with the owner. Every member was independent of the others and not compelled to attend meetings or mingle with others associated with the union; yet when a member neglects meetings, they were inclined to avoid the leader, even though the leader doesn't normally know who among the members regularly attends meetings.

The reason I reveal these cultural attributes is to expose the behaviors of the old that enabled the success of the past, and maybe provide a guide to the future. I had the privilege of interacting with some members of the group in a different capacity as a member of the staff, even though very young at the time; I was expected to be observant in the management of the business and especially in the absence of the owner. As I write, I may recall some events that could help in the course of our struggle. I viewed the respect accorded the leader by the members whenever he was present at the meetings as signs of gratitude for the free drinks, and nothing else was associated to it by me at the time. Little did I know that it was a way of life, a custom of the Igbo's, or that there were significances to it. As I have grown older in the post Nigeria-Biafra war, it's done on me that there was a great deal to it. I have often asked myself, what is the problem with the Igbo's? Why are they not united in the face of these multitudes of problems, individually and collectively? I have not found satisfactory answers yet.

But I have decided to reflect on the past and from that able to deduce wisdom in the ways of the old and the benefits they derived from their ways. I had often wondered within myself whether the situation with the Igbo's could be attributable to other factors, or is the war singly responsible for completely altering the behavior of the people to the point of totally absconding from their ways, or is there an inherent characteristic in the culture that was not apparent because of the determination and pragmatism of the leaders of the old? I fully understand there could be possible effects a cruel punishment can have on a people, but that would have been more destructive if it were totally unexpected. In this instance, the defeat of Biafra called for expectations of the worst, even though one can argue that a lesser punishment would have been appropriate, considering the involvement of Dr. Nnamdi Azikiwe in the negotiated settlement, and the fact that the former premier of the old Western region of Nigeria (Chief Obafemi Awolowo) was in jail in Biafra when the war started, and the Biafran leader could have dealt severely with him but didn't and instead secured his release with promises to return the favor, which never came. Prior experiences with the Western premier could have been a yardstick for measuring his trustworthiness, and as such a reason to have been better prepared.

I am not at all certain whether the signals during the Nigeria-Biafra war gave any clue to the leaders at the time of the dire consequences that could be emitted out to their citizens should they fail to wrestle themselves out of defeat. In retrospect, I must say that the actions of the former Nigerian president and premier of Eastern Nigeria, Chief Dr. Nnamdi Azikiwe, may have been intended to solve what he taught was an impending danger; and to that effect, his intervention was beneficial, without which the outcome could have been more devastating. This critique is not intended to coddle praises on any leaders of the Biafran era, but to bring forth the wisdom of the past with the intent of generating some thoughts among the leaders of the present and possible leaders of the future, but will not fail to reveal names of past leaders whose specific actions were worthy of the times and possible yardsticks of measurements for the leaders of the future, or reference points of emulation in the future.

Now, are there any failures on the actions of past leaders that will hinder us from welding ourselves together to be able to face the impending dangers of the future? I am reminded of the Eastern regional legislation that forbids the Osu cast system in Eastern Nigeria and, before that, the ability of the old to have realized that twin births was not a curse on a family but a blessing for a family. I have disclosed these two specific practices of pre Nigeria-Biafra war because I can't recall what Chief Dr. Nnamdi Azikiwe or Dr. Michael Okpara governments of former Eastern Nigeria did that could have set such an awful example for the present chrome of leaders who don't seem to get their acts right.

I have raised several questions in this commentary and will now attempt to answer a few.

Question: What is the problem with the Igbo's?

Answer: The Igbo's of nowadays are not the same with the Igbo's of the old. There was a saying among the non-Igbo's of pre Nigeria-Biafra war, that one should be careful to offer a helping hand to an Igbo, because if you do, the chances are that he will bring his brother next, and that brother will bring another brother next, and by the time you realize it, you have lost your property. The significance of this saying is that the Igbo's of the old were helpful to each other.

What is preventing the Igbo's of nowadays from adopting the same strategy? Can anyone sincerely say this practice continues to date?

I was talking with a lecturer from a local university recently, and the issue of former Governor Orji Kalu of Abia State cropped up. I listened very carefully to him, and his total argument was that Orji Kalu was not educated enough. I asked myself, when would God come to our aid? I asked this learned professor, which governor was better than Orji Kalu? He provided no answer. Orji Kalu has a steady record of pro-Igbo politics along the lines of Alvan Ikoku, Akanu Ibiam, Mbonu Ojike, Louis Mbanefo, Michael Okpara, Patrick Ottih, Odumegwu Ojukwu, Green Mbadiwe, Emeka Ojukwu, and Samuel Mbakwe. (With exceptions to the deaths of young Igbo leaders under his watch)

Governorship is a leadership position, not a university classroom; and once one assumes that position, he or she should be judged by performance in office. We should be looking at the development of the states; creation of environments conducive for development, infrastructure development, such as road construction; sighting of industries; payment of salaries to civil servants and teachers; provision of health services; improvement in education; beautification of environments; maintenance of roads; security in society, such as law and order enforcements etc. If a governor does well in these respects, he or she is a good governor. Forget about the level of education before assuming office—experience is education.

The reason I divulge names such as Alvan Ikoku, Akanu Ibiam, Mbonu Ojike, Louis Mbanefo, Michael Okpara, Patrick Ottih, Odumegwu Ojukwu, Green Mbadiwe, Emeka Ojukwu, Samuel Mbakwe, etc., is to expose the fortitude of great Igbo leaders whose sole interests were to promote the well-being of Igbo society and whose associations or relationships with other Nigerian leaders were determined by the interest of the group.

Now! Let's expose the affections of some of these leaders.

1. Question: Do you remember who financed NCNC?
   Answer: Sir Louis Odumegwu Ojukwu and Mazi Green Mbadiwe
2. Question: Do you know where the funds for the initial Biafran offensive came from?
   Answer: Sir Louis Odumegwu Ojukwu
3. Question: Do you know who financed Biafran diplomatic activities especially at the later stages of the war?
   Answer: Chief Patrick Nwakamma Ottih
4. Question: Can you tell the Igbo's and the world what level of education Patrick Ottih, Odumegwu Ojukwu and Green Mbadiwe had?

Conjecturably an Igbo octogenarian will provide an adequate answer.

Question: Why are the Igbo's not united in the face of these multitudes of problems, individually and collectively?

Answer: The Igbo's have been gripped with defeatist syndrome and have not risked their personal resources for the benefits of their people. Few Nigerian governments have been kind to the Igbo's, such as the Ibrahim Babangida and Sani Abacha administrations. No other administrations have given the Igbo's a free hand at managing the resources placed under their control; a typical example was the Olusegun Obasanjo-Ngozi Okonjo Iweala saga.

Governors and local governments chairpersons in the Southeast have not managed resources well either, and at this point it's difficult to know which direction to turn. I refuse to believe that the era of Dr. Michael OKpara, Chief Samuel Mbakwe, or of good governments in Igbo land is over. I am inclined to believe that good times will return; I wonder how the governors and local government chairmen who squandered our resources will be remembered. A few will remember Chris Ngige and Orji Kalu for their efforts; who are the rest? Can you remember? Some may be remembered for the deaths of aspiring Igbo leaders within their domain.

The Igbo's have completely forgotten how they arrived at their preeminent positions before the Nigeria-Biafra war. It was by economic empowerment and cultivation of the Igbo cultural attributes, such as assisting relatives and kinfolks in their entrepreneurial endeavors, creating opportunities in their respective communities through the availability of bank loans to small businesses, construction of mini-industries, such as private elementary and secondary schools, nursing schools, commercial colleges, medical centers, cottage homes. Also through food cultivations, which was assisted by the Michael Okpara administration. To put it in another form, the Igbo's must revisit their microeconomics systems to return to their preeminent position.

How does culture influence economics? The Igbo's are too individualistic to get obsessed by unproductive government programs or policies, such as the chieftaincy program and the autonomous community policy. My late father, Mazi Ugwumadu Ottih, was called Nni yi ukwu Ugwumadu, meaning "the father of the community," by the entire Awa community—no one called him otherwise. This was a man who repeatedly refused chieftaincy titles, but instead recommended others for one. No one noticed when those chieftaincy holders died. When Mazi Ugwumadu Ottih died, the town stood at a standstill, literally paralyzed for days unending until he was buried. The Igbo's remember achievements and honors the same. Who among you think any of the so-called Eze's or chiefs of autonomous communalities in Igbo land are building medical centers, child-care facilities, elementary schools, mini-industries, or anything else that would advance the development of their communities? Who would remember them?

Igbo leaders must return to the basics and lift themselves again alongside their people. I can understand the rush, but a prudent approach to this problem will ensure a lasting result than so far been exhibited by a few renegade Igbo's who have utterly sold their soul for the kobo. Let me ask you a question, is Olusegun Obasanjo an Igbo president? Can a true Igbo leader in the mold of our heroes, Alvan Ikoku, Akanu Ibiam, Mbonu Ojike, Louis Mbanefo, Michael Okpara, Patrick Ottih, Odumegwu Ojukwu, Emeka Ojukwu, Samuel Mbakwe, etc., cause the kind of atrocities that was witnessed in Anambra State, close down Slok Airlines or Sardana Bank and expect our people to applaud him?

Have you noticed something? Gani Fawehinmi, the famous and aggressive civil rights leader, whose record in Nigerian civil rights history was assured, became a stout defender of Olusegun Obasanjo's antidemocratic policies. It boggles the mind that at this stage in Nigerian history, the few who have held high moral grounds could succumb to ethnic sentiments. Obasanjo's anti-Igbo politics mirrors closely Awo's tenure as federal minister of finance, and yet many Igbo's are exceedingly uncertain which direction to turn.

Examine Nigeria's developmental pattern under Olusegun Obasanjo. How many industries were sighted in the old Eastern Nigeria or sold to People of the South East or South-South zone in Obasanjo's corrupt privatization scheme? Do you think the late Col. Anthony Ochefu, the first military governor of old East Central State of Nigeria, could have done better? His people are interested in Apa State with Nsukka as the capital. Does that mean anything to present-day Igbo leaders? Is Peter Odili any different from Orji Kalu, Sam Ngwu, Chris Ngige, Achike Udenwa, or Peter Obi? APGA was prepared to endorse him for the presidency and Ohaneze too. Ndoni his hometown was formerly part of the old Oguta county council and divisional council in the old Eastern region of Nigeria. Is he Igbo? Is Col. Anthony Ochefu Igbo?

We seem to have forgotten very quickly the late Mazi Mbonu Ojike's doctrine; he believed in a larger Eastern region of Nigeria and convinced Professor Eyo Ita and Earnest Okoli to join him—and they did. Only a large economic union can sustain our region. Please try to understand the plight of the Niger Delta. If you do, that will be comforting, and don't forget you are still neighbors, or are you planning to move to the North or the West? Do you belong to the Odu People's Congress or are you a Moslem?

The people of the Niger Delta are actually fighting a just cause; the resources in their land have not been utilized to their advantage. Some of their leaders who ask why are simply put away, and yet others seem to entertain the slogan, "The war was fought to prevent the Igbo's from seizing your oil." The Igbo's have been absent from Nigerian decision making process since the beginning of the Nigeria-Biafra war (1967-2008), and it's time for South-South leaders to ask Nigerian government leaders, what reasons they now have for the impoverished nature of the Niger Delta. And don't forget, Saka Boro and Ken Sara Wiwa were not killed by the Igbo's.

Alhaji Asari-Dokuba, a true freedom fighter, was left in jail for a while, while Dr. Adams of Odu People's Congress was freed. Does anyone think the struggle in the Niger Delta have not made a difference? Chief Ralph Uwazurike is now free as well, but don't forget both him and Alhaji Asari-Dokuba were freed under President Yar 'A'dua.

I get vexed when I remember that Obasanjo and his Igbo cronies easily evaded the home of Nnamdi Azikiwe, Odumegwu Ojukwu, Louis Mbanefo, Nwafor Arize, Chike Obi, C. C. Mojekwu, Emeka Ojukwu, Alex Ekwueme, Chuba Okadigbo, Kenneth Dike, Chinua Achebe, R. O. Nkwocha, Daniel Nwandu, and Augustine Ilodibe. Could the Igbo's have a spot where their honored ones could rest peacefully? Who is Andy Uba? Was he governor for two weeks? Was Chris Uba in jail? What a world. What a horrible time in Nigeria. The Obasanjo/Atiku era must be seen for what it was—a hideous time in Nigerian history.

I was attempting to answer the question, why are the Igbo's not united in the face of these multitudes of problems, individually and collectively? Did I really answer it?

Question: Is there an inherent characteristic in the culture that was not apparent because of the determination and pragmatism of the leaders of the old?

Answer: No, the Igbo's have always had a republican mentality and have had experiences like this in the past. One accident or the other had in previous times been attributed to their comeback. Their very last rebound was attributed to the insolence in the old Western Nigeria Regional Assembly.

The Igbo's have never had a homogenous society; Igbo towns and communities regard themselves as whole and always endeavored to have self-governments. Although similarities existed, there were plenty of differences as well. I was talking to a friend lately, a native of Owerri in Imo State of Nigeria, about the late Mazi Raymond Amanze Njoku, the former minister of transport in the old Eastern region of Nigeria. I was eager to know if he was of Aro origins (descendents of Aro-Chukwu in Abia State of Nigeria) because the Aro's are known to bear Mazi in their names. He said no. He informed me that Mazi was a title in Owerri culture. Such differences exist all over the Igbo nation. One obvious difference is the titles of original Igbo kings—the EZE-ARO of Aro-Chukwu, the OBI of Onitsha, the EZE-IGWE of Oguta, etc.

Those of us born in the '40s and '50s and perhaps '60s came across books that talked about Igbo village democracy. Common references are *Things Fall Apart* and *A Man of the People* by Chinua Achebe, who is still with us. These books symbolized the heroisms of individuals in various communities and didn't attempt to compare heroes of one community to the other—though that might have been deliberate. But generally, the Igbo's don't usually denigrate one another's culture. These differences in culture have always existed and

41

may never end. One general characteristic of Igbo village democracy is that the Igbo's have always honored their sons and leaders who improve their lives and promote the wellbeing of their communities.

My particular interest in pointing out these facts and part of which have driven my inscription is to bring forth the attributes of the past that must be emulated by the leaders of the future. I have shown eloquently in this article a desire to unveil names of leaders who, over the course of their lives, have had affection in promoting the welfare of the general Igbo population. Some of these names may be modestly known or not heard of outside their immediate Igbo towns and surrounding communities; because of the nature of Igbo societies and sometimes out of ignorance, people associate names that have been heard of frequently over the airwaves and mass media with greatness, without knowing what contributions these individuals have made in society if any. This commentary promotes substance, not propaganda. I beg to ask, have you read the book *The Trouble with Nigeria* by Chinua Achebe?

In 1978, as an executive member of Imo State branch of Great Nigerian Peoples Party, it wasn't prudent for me to attend a rally organized by Nigerian Peoples Party, but I seriously wanted to and decided to seek permission from an elderly executive, the late Chief A.U.D Mba from Mbieri. He didn't inquire from me why I needed to attend because he might have known. Chief Dr. Nnamdi Azikiwe was coming to Owerri and that was to be his first appearance in public as Nigeria prepares for the second republic or, in other words, his second coming to the Nigerian political scene.

I heard much of his contributions to Nigerian independence and sturdily craved to see the man in person, but it didn't turn out so well. There were several speakers before the honorable, all in praise of him; but when it came his turn to speak, he spoke exclusively about the late Mazi Mbonu Ojike. He talked of how good he was, how selfless he was, what contribution he made to Nigerian society, what he meant to the Igbo's, and on and on. I didn't know what to make of his speech, but to be honest to you; it didn't make much sense to me at the time. I wondered what sense it made to talk about a man who died in 1956 to an audience in 1978, who really hadn't heard much about him than "boycott the boycottables." When I left the rally, I returned to the offices of the blessed Chief A.U.D. Mba and narrated the story to him. After a moment, he said, "He might have been the best of his time." I left, not sure of all that had transpired that day.

As I grew older, I started researching about Mazi Mbonu Ojike, and today I have established an institute named after him—Mbonu Ojike Institute for Public Policy Research. Go to Mbonuojikeinstitute.com and read more.

Are you still with me? I was stating that I desire to expose the attributes of the past that must be emulated by the leaders of the future. I had earlier disclosed such names as Sir Louis Odumegwu Ojukwu. He was said to be the first African millionaire in West Africa, but his millions is important to my subject matter only because he used it to advance humanity. He contributed immensely to the progress of Nigerian society by realizing the importance of Nigerian self-rule, which led to his financing of the National Council of Nigeria and the Cameroon's and was assisted in that effort by the equally great Mazi Green Mbadiwe.

It will be wrong to talk of the successes of NCNC without remembering those that financed it. Sir Louis also played a role in the development of Eastern Nigeria by seeing to the employment of our young graduates through the establishment of Nkalagu cement industry. I equally revealed his assistance to Biafran itinerary. It should be of important historical note that his son, Chief Chukwuemeka Odumegwu Ojukwu, employed his resources for the benefits of the Igbo's. If not of our ability to defend ourselves at the initial stages of the Nigeria-Biafra war, only the heavens would have known what could have come of us. We thank him and his family.

It needs to be stated unambiguously that the presidential candidacy of Chief Dr. Nnamdi Azikiwe in 1979, less than ten years after the defeat of Biafra, was a blessing to the Igbo's. That campaign was made possible by the judicious mind of late Justice P. O. Balonwu of Onitsha and the philanthropy of former Senator Francis Arthur Nzeribe of Oguta. The Igbo's should thank all three.

This brings me to the subject of Chief Patrick Nwakamma Ottih. He was a Nigerian millionaire, resident in the Cameroon's City of Victoria, long before Nigeria achieved independence. He was a leading member of the Casablanca Group of the African Nationalist Movement; later he joined the National Council of Nigeria and the Cameroon's in Southern Cameroon and pushed for Southern Cameroon merger with Eastern Nigeria. He took up the mantle of Igbo leadership in the Cameroon Republic and served as the president of the Cameroon branch of the Igbo State Union for a considerable period of years until the Nigeria-Biafra war.

He formed the Biafra Movement in West Cameroon and used his association with the West Cameroon regional government to secure their backing for the Biafran war efforts and opened a Biafran embassy in Victoria City while the Cameroon national government supported Nigeria. He next got involved in Biafran diplomatic activities and refugees aid and spent millions of his own money for those purposes. He funneled capital to Biafran diehards who trained militant Biafrans on Cameroon soil, battling against Nigerian armed forces, attempting to break through to the Biafran side through the Calabar axis.

When the war ended, the Cameroon federal authorities swiftly apprehended him, arrested the entire leadership of his Biafran Movement, destroyed his business empire; but through the intervention of his friend, the vice president of the republic, Mr. Solomon Tandeng Muna, he was released and advised to run for his life. He returned to Nigeria, but slipped back to Cameroon's on two different occasions to dispose some worthy properties. He lived peacefully in Nigeria and died of old age on November 18, 2004, at the age of eighty-six, satisfied of his accomplishments and contributions in life. What do you make of him? Read more in his biography titled *Beyond the Biafran Shore*.

Question: I have in this article disclosed names of some remarkable Nigerian leaders. Why are they important?

Answer: They are important because they made a difference in Nigerian society and continue to make a difference to date. I have stated very distinctly my regard for Chief Ottih, Sir Louis and Mazi Mbadiwe. They are many others whose contributions through their choice of industries I will herein detail.

1. Dr. Alvan Ikoku of Aro-Chukwu—A towering figure in Nigerian politics. His image is in Nigerian currency, and yet he held few government positions in life. Proprietor, Aggrey Memorial College in Aro-Chukwu and today's Alvan Ikoku College of Education in Owerri. These two institutions have trained thousands of Igbo's and other Nigerians, whose contributions in Nigerian society can no longer be ascertained. In addition, he was the leader of the opposition in the Eastern Nigeria Regional assembly and chairman of the Biafran constituent assembly.

2. Chief G. E. Okeke of Ihiala—Member, Eastern Nigeria Regional Assembly; minister of production in Eastern Nigeria under Dr. Michael I. Okpara; proprietor, Abbot Boy's secondary school, Ihiala and Abbot Girl's secondary school, Ihiala, Anambra State, Nigeria. His choice of industry was of immense contributions to the development of his hometown and the surrounding communities.

3. Chief H. P. O. Udom of Oguta—First Imo State chairman of Nigerian Peoples Party; member, Eastern Nigeria Regional Assembly; proprietor, Trinity High School, Oguta, and Obiako Commercial College, Oguta. His place in the history of his town is yet to be rivaled. He was called

the insurmountable and regarded very highly in Oguta local government council and surrounding communities, because of his role in the development of Oguta town.

4. Dr. B. U. Nzeribe of Awomama—Vice presidential candidate of Nigeria under the platform of Great Nigerian People's party; deputy speaker of the Nigeria House of Representatives in the first republic; proprietor, Palm Beach Insurance and Palm Beach hotels in Nigeria; founder, Comprehensive Secondary School, Awomama; founder, Awomama General Hospital, and built a cathedral for his community. He brought his community to limelight, and he's highly regarded for those contributions.

5. Dr. Nnanna Ukaegbu of Imerinwe—Great Nigeria Peoples Party gubernatorial candidate in Imo State; founder, Owerri Grammar School, Imerinwe, Owerri; founder, Imo Technical University, Imerinwe, Owerri; founder, St. Basil Hospital, Amafor, Imerinwe, Owerri; founder, Imerinwe Girls Secondary School, Imerinwe, Owerri. Dr. Ukaegbu's contributions to the development of the Owerri metropolitan area and surrounding communities propelled his name within the state.

6. Chief G. C. Okoye of Ndoni—Chairman, East Central State Education Board, Member, Eastern Nigeria Regional Assembly; proprietor, St. Michael Secondary School, Osu-Obodo, Oguta local government council. His role in the development of one-half of the old Oguta divisional council helped the communities in that part of the locality advance their educational goals, and that reduced economic burdens on individual families.

7. Chief Ikenna Nzimiro of Oguta—A successful entrepreneur and former mayor of Port Harcourt City, Rivers State, Nigeria; proprietor, Priscilla Memorial Secondary School, Oguta, Imo State, Nigeria.

8. Chief L. N. Obioha of Aro-Ndizuogu—A successful industrialist and founder of Ndizuogu farms, a large palm tree plantation and palm oil and kernel processing plant in Aro-Ndizuogu, Orlu, Imo State, Nigeria

9. Chief F. U. Anyanwu of Mbaise—Founder, Fuason Industries, an aluminum sheet metal manufacturing plant in Owerri, Imo State, Nigeria

10. Chief Patrick Nwakamma Ottih of Awa—A successful entrepreneur and proprietor of Ottih Brothers departmental stores, and Ottih Brothers radio and electrical departments; founder, Awa Community Secondary School, Awa; founder, Awa Progressive Welfare Association, through which he awarded scholarships to deserving and low-income students of Awa Community Secondary School, and sponsored trophies for sports competitions in Oguta county council, Oguta divisional council, and Ohaji/Egbema/Oguta local government council area schools.

11. Sir Louis Odumegwu Ojukwu of Nnewi—A renowned industrialist and founder of Nkalagu cement industry, Nkalagu. Founder of several wharf—affiliated companies in Lagos State, Nigeria

12. Mazi Green Mbadiwe of Aro-Ndizuogu—A successful entrepreneur and founder of a coal mining industry in Kaduna State, Nigeria.

Others with equally impressive entrepreneurial accomplishments are Chief John Ihekwoaba of Nkwere, Chief Abaecheta of Mbieri, Chief Nnanna Kalu of Abiriba, Chief Okonkwo Kano of Nnewi, Chief Ruben O. Nkwocha of Enugu-ukwu, Chief Augustine Ilodibe of Nnewi, Chief Francis Ihekwoaba of Nkwere, Chief Daniel Nwandu of Enugu-ukwu, and Chief Christian C. Onoh of Enugu.

All the above names were selected due to their contributions to the development of education in their respective communities, successful entrepreneurial attainments that elevated their status in Igbo society, or abilities to provide employments to their relevant populations—because wealth devoid of economic utility to industrious communities or secluded from normal economic activities in neighboring populations or prevented from economic benefits to adjacent vicinities amounts to economic stagnation of communities or subjection of human populations to economic adversity. Each individual in a position to help should assist the less fortunate in his or her community as to advance humanity. This was the method adopted by the Igbo's in developing their society, advancing their educational goals while maintaining their republican mentality.

Note for Posteriority

Chief Patrick Nwakamma Ottih (1918-September 18, 2004) was a consummate Igbo ideologue and business magnate, who was a participant in the African Nationalist Movement, the Southern Cameroon independence struggles, and the Biafran secession struggles, through his leadership in the Casablanca Group, the National Council of Nigeria and the Cameroon's in Southern Cameroon, the Kamerun National Congress, the Cameroon Peoples' National Convention, the Igbo State Union, the Biafran Movement—relief efforts, and diplomatic activities.

On his burial, this note was posted

The Passage of a Legend
And
An Igbo Icon

As is often the case, any nation that could not hold its territory, never has its heroes immortalized. That is the case with the leaders who made the struggle for the Republic of Biafra possible.

Igbo leaders are hereby informed of the passing of this illustrious son who was a great financier of the Republic of Biafra, the son who provided a secretariat for the Biafran government in a foreign land and catered to its diplomats.

The giant whose towering personality and dogged determination helped split the policy position of the West Cameroon government from that of its national government, and had the West Cameroon government support the Biafran cause.

The icon that was at the center of much of the diplomatic activities of the Biafran government, and was part of the delegation, that toured world capitals seeking recognitions for the Republic of Biafra.

This person is Chief Patrick Nwakamma Ottih, also known as Ottih of Africa.

Glorious Exit

St Michaels' Cathedral Church
Aro-Awa Oguta LGA
Imo State

References

Madiebo, Alexander A. 1980. *The Nigeria revolution and the Biafran war.* Fourth Dimension Publishers.

Arthur Nwankwo, "The Igbo leadership and the future of Nigeria," Fourth dimension publishers 1985

Ben Gbulie, "The fall of Biafra" the new frontiers in publishing, 1989

Bernard Odogwu, "No place to hide, (crises and conflicts inside Biafra" 1985

Chinua Achebe, "The Trouble with Nigeria" fourth dimensions publishers

Mazi Ngozi Ottih, "Beyond the Biafran Shore" Xlibris Corporation, 2008

Ntieyong U. Akpan, "The struggle for secession" Frank Cass and company, 1976

Obi, Chike "Our Struggle" fourth dimension publishers, 1986

Raphael Chijioke Njoku "African cultural values: Igbo political leadership in colonial Nigeria; History, Politics, Economics and culture" 2006.

Articles

Igbo 101: Facts little told, by Ogaranya Uju Nkwocha Afulezi Ph D

Incongruencies in Modern Igbo government, by Ihechukwu Chiedozie Madubuike, Ph D, D litt

An Eastern Reunion, by Obi Nwakanma, Vanguard 2001

West Africa and colonialism, part 3 by Wendy McElroy, Jan.10 2005

Cameroon elections, by Tessy D. Bakery

Developing political leadership in Ala Igbo, by Ozodi Thomas Osuji, Ph. D

Eteng and the Igbo, by P.J. Ezeh

Web sites

www.biafrafoundation.com
www.cameroonincolour.com

Organizations

Seattle—Limbe Friendship Association
Mbonu Ojike Institute for Public Policy Research

www.ingramcontent.com/pod-product-compliance
Lightning Source LLC
Chambersburg PA
CBHW061224280526
45784CB00006B/2621